DA 445.m6

NIKOLAUS PEVSNER

CHRISTOPHER WREN

1632 - 1723

UNIVERSE BOOKS, NEW YORK

First American Edition
published in the United States of America in 1960 by

UNIVERSE BOOKS, INC.
381 Park Avenue South
NEW YORK 16, NEW YORK

Library of Congress Catalog Card Number 60-12418
© Electa Editrice 1960

Printed in Italy

Christopher Wren was born in 1632 in the village of East Knoyle in Wiltshire. His father was a parson and was soon promoted to be dean of the Royal Chapel at Windsor replacing his brother who then became bishop of Ely. When the boy was ten, the Civil War broke out. The Wrens were a royalist family; the Bishop of Ely was in fact so anti-puritan that he had already been arrested in 1641 and confined to the Tower of London. There he remained until 1661. Meanwhile the Dean of Windsor retired to his son-in-law, Christopher's brother-in-law, who was also a parson. Both father and brother-in-law had scientific leanings and were interested in architecture. The father annotated his edition of Sir Henry Wotton's *Elements of Architecture*, the first book in English on architectural theory. The brother-in-law wrote a Treatise on *The Natural Grounds and Principles of Harmony*, including in it those parallels between harmonic musical and visual proportions which had been so dear to Italian humanists. He is supposed to have introduced Christopher to mathematics. Christopher was a precocious child indeed. He went as a boarder to Westminster School in London, at the same time that Dryden, the poet, and John Locke, the philosopher (born in 1631 and 1632 respectively) were there. When at school he built a model of the relationships of sun, moon and earth and gave it to his father with a Latin poem. At the age of fifteen he translated into Latin the chapter on sundials from Oughtred's *The Key to Mathematics* and Oughtred, in the Latin edition of 1652, called *Clavis Mathematicae*, referred to this translation. This work Wren undertook for Charles Scarburgh, and in the next year Wren helped Scarburgh with dissections at Surgeon's Hall. He also designed a ceiling with figures of Geometry and Astronomy and invented a pen which made it possible to write in duplicate.

In 1649, or perhaps a little earlier, he went up to Oxford and then took his B.A. in 1651, his M.A. in 1653. In 1657 he was made Professor of Astronomy at Gresham College in London, a college in the City which had been founded under Queen Elizabeth I. He had to lecture there in Latin as well as English. His Inaugural Lecture is a remarkable document, partly for his resolute plea for the application of science to practical purposes such as time-measuring and navigation, partly for such progressive proposals as the compilation of complete meteorological records, and partly for such prophetic remarks as the one in which he says that « every nebulous star » may be « the Firmament of some other world. »

Wren, the scientist, was highly appreciated by scientists both in England and on the Continent. Oughtred in 1652 praised his *praeclarum ingenium* and his many *praeclara inventa*, John Evelyn called him « that miracle of a youth, » when he first met him in 1654, and Isaac Newton much later named him as one of the three *huius aetatis facile principes*. Robert Hooke, his friend, said of him that « there scarce ever met in one man, in so great a perfection, such a mechanical hand, and so philosophical a mind. » And Pascal, who some times challenged foreign scholars by putting problems to them, wrote of Wren's solution to one of them: « Il n'y a rien de plus beau que ce qui a été envoyé par M. Wren. » In 1661 Wren was made Professor of Astronomy at Oxford.

Those were the years in which the Royal Society

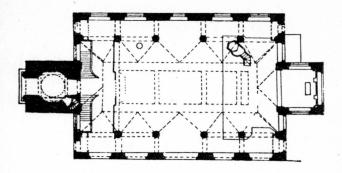

a) *St. James Garlickhithe (damaged, being restored).*

developed from a private club — called by Boyle, the great chemist, the « invisible college » — to a society with a royal charter. The group of the future founders of the Royal Society were Wren's friends and contemporaries. It was indeed he who wrote the preamble to the charter of the society.

Scientists in the seventeenth century were highly versatile. Specialization was to come later. Often the fruitful stands next to the futile, serious investigation next to toys. Wren in the years before 1660 invented and investigated an unbelievable number of things. John Evelyn saw in his rooms a speaking statue, a monstrous magnet and transparent beehives « built like palaces and castles. »

Parentalia, the biography written by Wren's son and published by his grandson, records fifty-three theories, inventions, experiments and mechanic improvements. They and other evidence we have include practical inventions such as a new way of embroidery for bedhangings, and a mechanism to weave seven pairs of stockings at the same time. They also include highly valuable medical experiments in blood transfusion, and « a new way to purge and vomit. » And they include matters of astronomy and mathematics such as a theory on the rings of Saturn, a theory on the pressure of the moon on the atmosphere of the earth, and research into the rectification of cycloids.

But they include a reference also to « New Designs tending to Strength, Convenience, and Beauty in Building » and several references to fortification and the attack of fortifications. Indeed, in 1661, when monarchy had been restored and Charles II, the new King, had married a Portuguese princess, Wren received a letter, written by his cousin who was private secretary to the Lord Chancellor, inviting him to go to Tangiers and inspect and improve the fortifications there. There was nothing strange from the point of view of the seventeenth century in a scientist or indeed any amateur appearing as an architect or engineer. Architecture had ceased to be a mason's trade with the end of the Middle Ages. Giotto designed the Campanile at Florence, Brunelleschi was a goldsmith, Alberti was an amateur, Bramante and Raphael were painters, Michelangelo was a sculptor. The corresponding change in England came later. Inigo Jones, the greatest English architect before Wren, had begun as a painter. It is characteristic in this context that it as Inigo Jones who transplanted to England the architectural system of the Italian Renaissance. Renaissance forms in details had been taken over ever since about 1510, but they were soon acclimatized, and the Elizabethan and Jacobean styles are as English as any of the Middle Ages. No one before Inigo Jones understood the world of Italian architecture in its entirety and endeavored to erect Italian buildings on English soil. The Queen's House or Villa at Greenwich (Pl. 57), begun in 1616, was the first, the Banqueting House in

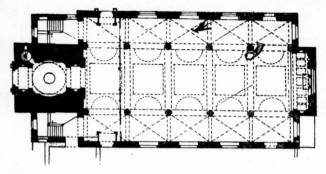

b) *St. Bride, Fleet Street (burned in 1940, being restored).*

the Royal Palace of Whitehall in London, begun in 1619, the second. They established the superiority of classical canons which could only be learned by going to Italy or studying the illustrated treatises of Serlio and Palladio.

At first the public and even men near the Court were baffled by this new style. « Some curious device » by Inigo Jones is what John Chamberlain called the Queen's House in 1617. It took more than a generation to acclimatize these innovations. Only a few followed Inigo Jones immediately, especially his nephew and assistant John Webb and a few amateurs such as Sir Roger Pratt. Jones himself built little. His greatest plan was never carried out, a large palace for the King at Whitehall. The ideas, based on French as much as Italian work, were taken up by Charles II. Jones was then dead, but Webb lived. He was not luckier than Jones. Again nothing materialized. A big new palace near London was begun instead, at Greenwich in 1663. It was soon discontinued. But it confirmed the classical style of

Jones as the style at the court, and it was, with its giant columns and pilasters and its heavy attic more Baroque and less Palladian than Jones' had been.

Yet it was not Webb but Professor Wren who was asked by Charles II about 1664 or 1665 to report on the condition of St. Paul's Cathedral, the large, partly Norman, partly Gothic cathedral in the City of London which had been refaced by Inigo Jones along its nave and aisles and its aisled transepts and, in addition, had been provided with a splendid deep portico of eight giant Corinthian columns, flanked by angle pillars — fifty feet tall and carrying a straight entablature without pediment and the statues of James I and Charles I. Charles II was interested in art as well as science. The charter of the Royal Society was granted by him. Wren made for him a model of the moon and gave him drawings of small insects as seen in a microscope. Charles knew well who he was — the son as well as nephew of trusted royalist churchmen. Moreover, the report on St. Paul's was to be concerned with structural rather than aesthetic questions. Finally however, Wren had by 1664 and 1665 indeed appeared on the scene as an architect.

In April 1663 he submitted to the Royal Society a model of the first building designed by him, the Sheldonian Theatre at Oxford (Pl. 2), given by Sheldon, his friend, as a ceremonial hall in order to disencumber the university church of functions of a similar nature. It is true that what made Wren assume an interest among the fellows of the Royal Society in this model was less its architecture than the constructional device he had worked out for the ceiling, which was to be of timber and have a span of 68 feet without intermediate supports. But the architecture of the building was also his. It was Roman and less inspired by Inigo Jones than by Serlio and Palladio. The façade has two

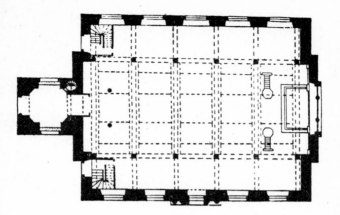

c) *St. James, Piccadilly (restored after 1945).*

superimposed orders of attached columns on the pattern of such buildings as the Theatre of Marcellus, the pediment with the half-pediments over the lower side pieces comes straight from Palladio's church façades and the shape of the building, oblong with an added semi-circle probably from Barbaro's edition of Vitruvius. The ceiling was painted with many figures but treated as if it were a canvas awning stretched across a building open to the sky. This feature especially established Wren's intention of being Roman.

At exactly the same time Wren designed a new chapel for Pembroke College at Cambridge. The chapel was a thank offering of his uncle who had been released from the Tower in 1661. It is equally classical in design. It has a simple front to the street with giant pilasters and a pediment, and a lantern on the roof above. The sources are again Italian, Serlio's « Temple at Tivoli » and perhaps a temple front in Cesariano's edition of Vitruvius. The chapel was completed in 1665, the Sheldonian Theatre in 1669. By then Wren had been appointed Surveyor General of the King's Works, which is the highest architectural job in the Kingdom.

How could that be, with men so much better trained and so much more experienced, such as John Webb, being available? The answer lies in Wren's development in the years immediately following the design for these first two buildings. In 1665 a plague raged in London. Wren left England and went on a nine-months' visit to Paris. From the only surviving letter, addressed to an Oxford friend, it is clear that he regarded architecture and architectural decoration as the prime object of this journey. Of course he met scientists too, and was evidently accepted as their equal, but his report is all about buildings, engravings, carving, plastering, gilding, and so on. He calls Paris « a School of Architecture, the best probably, at this Day in Europe. » He says that for a while the Louvre was his daily object of study. He reports that Bernini, just at that moment working in Paris on his vast schemes for a new Louvre, let him see his designs only for a few minutes. He refers to Mansart (whose Louvre designs and designs for a centrally planned Bourbon Chapel he seems to have been familiar with), to Levau's Collège des Quatre Nations, to the Palais Mazarin, to Versailles, of which he disliked the brick and stone parts built under Louis XIII, to Levau's Vaux-le-Vicomte and Mansart's Maisons Lafitte, which he calls incomparable, to St. Maur, Verneuil and many others.

However, what seems to have impressed him more than anything else is the domes which he could see in Paris. He had never seen any before except in illustrations. It must never be forgotten that he did not know Italy and never visited it later either. The only dome complete at the time was that of Mansart's church of the Visitation, but the domes of the Sorbonne and the Val de Grâce were nearly complete, and that of the Sorbonne could be also studied in engravings.

Wren returned to London in March or April 1666. In May his report on St. Paul's was delivered and this contained as its chief suggestion the building of a dome over the medieval crossing of the cathedral. It would have been a hazardous and an aesthetically unsatisfactory undertaking, but the design (Pl. 22) contained the germ of one of the most splendid features of Wren's own future rebuilding of St. Paul's: the widening of the domed space to a diameter, not equal to that of the nave and the naves of transept and chancel as in the crossing towers and crossing domes of medieval cathedrals, but to that of nave and aisles together in all four directions. The idea may have come to Wren from his knowledge of the fourteenth century crossing at Ely, though he may also have been familiar with such Italian buildings as Pavia Cathedral and Loreto. The dome was to have two shells with an opening from the inner into the outer, on the pattern of the Sorbonne or of Mansart's staircase at Blois. The proportions of the dome are very steep on an excessively tall drum with dangerously tall and closely set windows. It was an awkward design, and the facing of the Norman nave arcade with a big gallery by a system of giant pilasters was no more accomplished. The nave was however going to be vaulted by saucerdomes and penetrations from the upper windows, and this again became the system adopted for the new cathedral.

The reason why a new St. Paul's was necessary is the Fire of London, the fire which raged for three days in September 1666 and destroyed three-quarters of the City. The fire completed Wren's conversion from a scientist to an architect. He remained nominally professor at

Oxford until 1673, although as early as 1662 the Vice-Chancellor had complained of his absences.

The first thing he did, only a few days after the Fire, was to submit to the King a design for the replanning of London (Pl. 1). The plan was an immediate reaction to what he had seen in Paris. It is based in its essentials on the principle of the rond-point with radiating streets. The motif is repeated six times. It had been introduced in Paris under Henri IV, in the design of the never executed Place de France. Engravings of this were available. The center was to be — typical of London — not a palace nor a cathedral but the Royal Exchange. St. Paul's Cathedral was to be placed at the junction of two of the main streets, in a position similar to that of the Rainaldi churches in the Piazza del Popolo in Rome. The parish churches were all going to be resituated along the main streets.

So radical a change was clearly impossible. It would have presupposed a complete redistribution of property and for that there were neither the precise records in the City archives nor was there the time. Others, for instance Wren's friends, John Evelyn and Robert Hooke had also made plans, but they were no less unrealistic. So in the end the City was rebuilt very much as it had been before.

But if Wren could not create a new London in plan he did create a new skyline of London, the skyline which remained essentially unchanged into the nineteenth century. It was articulated and punctuated by the steeples of the parish churches. Of these 108 had existed before the fire, 87 were destroyed, 50 were rebuilt. Every one of these was designed by Wren who had been made first one of the three Royal Commissioners for the rebuilding of London (with Sir Roger Pratt and Hugh May — the City also nominated three, among them Hooke), and then put in charge of the control of the new church buildings. In addition to the fifty he designed four outside the City — a prodigious total. He was also very soon consulted on St. Paul's. But there a temporary solution was first suggested (1668). A choir and an « auditory » were to be built within the ruined old walls. Then these collapsed and Wren began to design a new building. In his plan for London the auditory was oblong, the chancel circular. So he started again at once with the conception of a dome. After that he worked on a strange oblong scheme with an arcade, which opened to the outside instead of the inside and a gallery over it, which opened in the traditional medieval way to the inside. With this scheme 1670 at the earliest is reached. In that year also a tax on coal was introduced to finance the building of the cathedral, of the parish churches and also of a monument to commemorate the Plague. However, work on the cathedral was still delayed for a while. But in 1670 seventeen of the new parish churches were started.

Contemplating their design, Wren was now clearly committed to the architectural profession, and we can understand now how it came about that Charles II made him Surveyor General in 1669. In the same year he got married. His wife died young in 1675. He married again in 1677 but was again unfortunate. From 1680 he remained a widower. He had three sons and a daughter. The daughter, his favorite, died at twenty-six. Only one son survived him. We know little of his character or private life. He was modest, not ambitious, not keen on publishing the results of his scientific research or on insisting on his authorship for the buildings he designed. He was small, graceful and alert, sociable and courteous, and as ingenious as a designer as he was skillful as a draftsman.

The City Churches are a creative effort to which there is hardly a parallel in Europe, although few of them are spectacular and only one can vie in spatial intricacy with the best of the seventeenth century in Rome. To understand them one must remember that Wren was an experimental scientist before he turned architect, and that his mind remained that of the scientist. He analyzed the program which would be valid for all these parish churches and then, as a true experimenter, demonstrated the maximum variety of solutions that can be obtained. The program, as he finally formulated it about 1708 is that an Anglican church must be primarily an « auditory, » in contrast to a Catholic church in which it is enough to hear « the murmur of te mass » and see the raising of the host. This conception of the post-tridentine Catholic church was faulty. But the conception of the protestant church was right.

We must now turn to the City churches and analyze them in some detail, first their plans, then their façades, and in the end their steeples. The plans of nearly all of them * fall into one of two categories: longitudinal or central, and there are many transitions between them.

The longitudinal is the most usual plan, a plan with nave and aisles in the Gothic tradition. Columns replace piers, a change made already in ecclesiastical architecture before Wren (e.g. the Salisbury Chapel at Hatfield, 1618) and groined vaults or tunnel vaults replace the open roofs of English Gothic. Wren may have known engravings of the Jesuit Church at Antwerp of 1615-1621 with its galleries, two orders of columns, and big tunnel vault. The rhythm from W to E varies a great deal according to whether bays are broad and few (St. Maryle-Bow) or narrow and many (St. Andrew Holborn, seven bays, St. Sepulchre, a remodeling of a Gothic church,

(*) The churches are here discussed regardless of whether they still exist. 25 were pulled down in the eighteenth to twentieth centuries, and 19 were damaged or destroyed in the Second World War. But most of these are under restoration or will be restored.

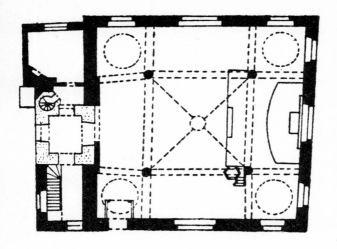

d) *St. Anne and St. Agnes (damaged in 1940).*

seven bays, Christ Church Newgate Street, six bays).
Moreover naves can have groined vaults (St. Michael
Cornhill, Christ Church) or tunnel vaults (St. Mary-le-
Bow, St. James Piccadilly [Pl. 5], St. Bride, St. Andrew
Holborn, etc.) or even a flat ceiling (St. Sepulchre).
Aisles may have groined vaults (St. Sepulchre, St. Michael
Cornhill, St. Clement Danes, etc.) transverse tunnel
vaults (St. Mary-le-Bow, St. Peter Cornhill), a composi-
tion influenced by Serlio's illustration of the Basilica
of Maxentius in Rome, or flat ceilings (Christ Church).
Then clerestories can be present or absent (St. Andrew
Holborn, St. James Piccadilly). If they are present, their
windows may be of many shapes, e.g. segment-headed
(St. Mary-le-Bow), or oval (St. Bride, St. Magnus [Pl.

6]). Finally the division between nave and aisles may be by two orders (St. Andrew Holborn, St. James Piccadilly, St. Clement Danes and St. Peter Cornhill, where pillars with attached pilasters are used) or by one giant order (St. Mary-le-Bow, St. Bride, St. Sepulchre, Christ Church), and orders may of course be Doric or Ionic or Corinthian. The only more radical difference from the current longitudinal plan is St. Clement Danes, which instead of the traditional English straight E end has an ambulatory and a semicircular E Chapel, influenced perhaps by the previous and ultimately by the Norman church which stood on this site.

There are far fewer strictly centrally planned City churches — indeed only five — perhaps because, owing to the rarity of such types in the English Middle Ages, the church authorities did not like them (cf. the story of St. Paul's, below). The five can be grouped as follows: St. Mary Abchurch (Pl. 7) is a square with a circular dome over, St. Swithin is a square with an octagonal domical vault over. The other three follow a type of venerable age, the inscribed cross, which goes back to the Early Christian centuries (e.g. Tarrasa in Catalonia, 6th century), exists in Byzantine architecture, appears in Italy in the 9th century (S. Satiro, Milan), became popular in Milan and Venice with the Renaissance (S. Giovanni Crisostomo, Venice) and then went to Holland. It is probably from the Nieuwe Kerk at Haarlem that Wren took the motif. It is a square with a square vaulted center on four free-standing columns, four equal cross arms, and lower vaulted or flat bays in the four corners. At St. Martin Ludgate (1677 etc.) the detail is exactly as at Haarlem, groin-vaulted center, tunnel-vaulted arms, flat-ceilinged corner bays. At St. Anne and St. Agnes (1676 etc.) the corner bays have saucer-domes. At St. Mary-at-Hill (1670 etc.) the center is domed.

But from the European point of view the most

characteristic problem of church design in the 17th century is neither the longitudinal nor the central plan, but combinations of the two, an interaction that endeavors to unite the monumentality of the central plan with the dynamics of the longitudinal plan. In Italy and France and later in Germany the symbol of this tendency, a typically Baroque tendency, is the oval. Wren in his most interesting plans is a European in this sense. He does not often make use of the oval, but combinations of longitudinal with central elements fascinate him as much as Bernini or Levau or Neumann. Examples can again be divided into two groups: central plans elongated, and longitudinal plans centralized.

First central plans elongated: St. Mildred Bread Street was a plain parallelogram and had a saucer-dome above the center and short tunnel-vaulted bays divided off to the E and W by arches on corbels, St. Antholin was an elongated octagon with an elongated octagonal center on columns and an oval dome, St. Benet Fink was an elongated decagon with an elongated hexagonal center on columns and an oval dome with a lantern.

Then longitudinal plans centralized: St. James Garlickhithe is of five bays with a coved ceiling. The aisles are narrow, the arcade has giant columns and a straight entablature. But for the middle bay the entablature turns to the outer walls, thus forming a central transept rising to the height of the nave ceiling. Similarly at St. Mary Aldermanbury the nave has five bays. It is tunnel-vaulted, but the middle bay has a groined vault as the bay of intersection with a tunnel-vaulted transept. The type is a descendant, but not a copy, of the Keyser's Westerkerk in Amsterdam.

St. Stephen Walbrook (Pl. 9), begun in 1672, is the most complex case and one which can be regarded as a trying-out of some elements for St. Paul's. It is longitudinal but has a large dome with lantern lighting.

The dome is intersected by the nave and chancel axis as well as a transeptal cross-axis. But the dome is much wider than the width of the arms and stands on a square of twelve columns. To gain the bottom circle of the dome eight arches are built up, four over nave, chancel, and transept ends, and four diagonally. The outer corner bays moreover are treated as at St. Mary-at-Hill.

Wren, as has been seen, was not shy of making use of foreign architects' ideas. So if he kept away from the Gesù type, he must have had reasons. One was perhaps that it seemed too exclusively Catholic, the other that it was indeed unsuitable as an auditory, because the chapels were excluded from direct communication with pulpit and altar.

Of façades much less need be said. The most awkward of the planning problems for Wren was the irregular shape of many of the sites. So in plenty of cases there was no scope for façades. At St. Mary-le-Bow and St. Stephen Walbrook he intended a loggia or colonnade by the side of the main entrance, but neither was carried out. East façades are usually more monumental or formal than west sides. They may simply be a wall with a pediment and a large window (St. Olave Jewry, where the window is of the Palladio type). They may be tripartite with only a window in the center (St. Stephen Coleman Street) or with windows in the side parts as well (St. Bride). The three parts may be under one pediment (St. Mary-at-Hill) or the center may be raised, plainly (St. Bride) or with the intercession of volutes (St. Anne and St. Agnes, St. Mary Aldermanbury [Pl. 11]) or of half-pediments of the kind used by Palladio (St. Andrew-by-Wardrobe, St. Mary Pattens). There may also be pilasters as an additional enrichment (St. Dionys Backchurch). Finally the windows may be treated as one monumental row, evenly spaced. There may be three

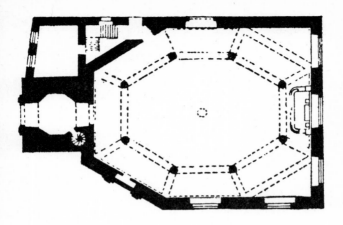

e) *St. Antholin, Watling Street (demolished in 1874).*

of them (St. Michael Wood Street) or five (St. Matthew Friday Street, and, with separate pilasters between, St. Peter Cornhill [Pl. 10]). West towers may project or be reduced to turrets rising over the center bay of the front (St. Edmund, St. Martin Ludgate Hill).

The steeples must have given Wren the keenest pleasure. They were certainly what was most admired by the visitor to London. « Londra è il paese dei bei campanili, » wrote Count Algarotti in 1753. He knew only one steeple in Italy worthy of a comparison. Wren's own pleasure, here as in the plans, was no doubt less in the aesthetics of outline and proportions than in the scope the steeples gave him for the systematic development of a large variety of types. We can distinguish seven types. They are, going from the simplest to the most complex, as follows: the plain square tower with parapet (St. Andrew-by-the-Wardrobe, St. Clement Eastcheap), the same type with pinnacles (St. Andrew Holborn, St. Mary Somerset with eight pinnacles, and the Gothic towers of St. Alban Wood Street, St. Mary Aldermary, St. Michael Cornhill), the same with a small lantern (St. Anne and St. Agnes, St. Mary Aldermanbury), the same with a dome and a lantern (St. Benet Paul's Wharf, i.e. the Welsh church). Then there are a small number of spires entirely in continuation of Gothic precedent (St. Antholin, St. Margaret Pattens, St. Swithin) and there is one example of a Gothic steeple: St. Dunstan-in-the-East (Pl. 21), where the spire is carried on four steep flying buttresses thrown up diagonally from four pinnacles, on the pattern of the former Gothic spire of St. Mary-le-Bow (Pl. 13). On these Gothic designs of Wren's more must be said later.

The most usual type of Wren steeple is that with an obelisk spire. At St. Nicholas Cole Abbey the obelisk was short and rested immediately on the square. At St. Edmund it stands on an octagonal lantern, at St. Lawrence Jewry on a square lantern. At St. Peter Cornhill and St. Magnus (Pl. 15) a cupola is interposed between lantern and obelisk. St. Mildred Bread Street had a concave-sided cupola, St. Mary Abchurch and St. Martin Ludgate (Pl. 16) have ogee-sided cupolas. Finally there are eight more ingenious designs, all late in Wren's development, and to these must be added, as a crowning achievement, the W towers of St. Paul's. They all have stone-lanterns of more than one story. They are the following: First three small, recessed ones with specially playful detail: St. Stephen Walbrook (Pl. 17), St. James Garlickhithe (Pl. 4), and St. Michael Paternoster Royal (Pl. 18). The first two are square, the third is octagonal. Then there is the octagonal spire of St. Bride (Pl. 12), a design developed entirely from one motif, repeated five times, telescoped, and reduced in height as it goes up higher. It is more ingenious than aesthetically successful. Christ Church Newgate Street (Pl. 14) has as its principal effect a very noble colonnade of free-standing columns against the lantern stage. St. Mary-le-Bow has in the same place a rotunda of free-standing columns. St. Michael Crooked Lane was an essay with a circular core like that of St. Mary-le-Bow, but garnished chiefly with volutes. But the most Baroque of all are St. Vedast Foster Lane (Pl. 19) with no columns at all but a Borrominesque contrast between a first concave-sided and a second convex-sided stage of the spire, and the W towers of St. Paul's, where the sequence is convex-concave instead of concave-convex, and ample use is made in addition of columns set diagonally.

But the towers of St. Paul's Cathedral were not designed until several years after 1700, at a time when Wren was over eighty years old. He was forty-three when the foundation stone was laid. The design on which a beginning was then made has a remarkable prehistory. In the summer of 1673, after the preliminary stages referred to were over, Wren had embarked on a very bold and uncompromising design (Pl. 23, 24) — a Greek cross with broad concave quadrant curves to connect the arms (a motif derived from Antoine Lepautre's book of 1652) and with a dominant dome over the center surrounded by an ambulatory consisting of circular bays in the diagonals and square bays enlarged by two apses each in the main directions. The source of this is probably Bramante's St. Peter as illustrated by Serlio rather than S. Giovanni dei Fiorentini or Mansart's Bourbon Chapel. A model was then made, a fine large piece of joinery 18 feet in size, which still exists. Here the Greek cross is enlarged by a lower domed West bay and a large detached giant portico of eight columns at the west end — somewhat on the lines of

Sangallo's modification of Bramante's St. Peter's. The Great Model (Pl. 25), as it is called, was, we know, Wren's ideal of a major church.

However it did not please the clergy. They wanted a cathedral, as Old St. Paul's had been, and not a temple after the new fashion. It may seem surprising that Wren was quite ready to oblige them, and he now produced, some time in 1674, a completely different and unquestionably inferior design. This is indeed essentially like a Norman cathedral, with a nave with aisles, far projecting transepts with aisles and a long chancel with aisles. The only thing on which Wren insisted was the wide domed space at the crossing, again, as in the design of before the Fire, as wide as nave and aisles together, though now on an octagonal plan and no longer a square plan with angle niches as it had been in the pre-Fire design. But even here he compromised and proposed a tall thin spire on top of his dome, an awkward — one is tempted to say an absurd — shape. Yet this was approved by the clergy and received the Royal Warrant in May 1675. Wren was knighted shortly before this.

If Wren had obviously agreed to a compromise, King and Clergy also agreed to one — an eminently English procedure. The warrant says that Wren was to erect the building according to the warrant design but with « the liberty, in the execution of his work, to make some variation, rather ornamental than essential, as from time to time he should see proper. » This he did, and although work started in 1675 in accordance with the warrant design, alterations began almost at once and culminated in the great dome which is one of the most nearly perfect ever designed in any country and has almost nothing in common with the monstrosity of the warrant design.

In describing St. Paul's Cathedral (Pl. 27, 33) the following features deserve special emphasis. The walls

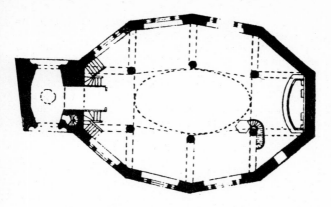

f) *St. Benet Fink (demolished in 1843).*

are treated in two stories with coupled pilasters between
the wide window bays. The system is developed from
that of Inigo Jones' Banqueting House. But the whole
upper story is a sham, a screen wall to hide the fact
that the aisles are much lower than the nave and that
the nave vaults are abutted by flying buttresses, entirely
in the Gothic way. The screen walls also act as a
welcome abutment to the dome at the corners of nave
and transepts, and transepts and chancel. The transept
façades have the enrichment of semicircular porticoes
on the pattern of Pietro da Cortona's at S. Maria della
Pace. The west front is two-storied and has the two
towers already mentioned. The two stories are given
loggias with coupled columns, and here St. Louis des
Invalides and Perrault's colonnade of the Louvre were
the godparents. But Wren's columns curiously interlocked
with the bases of the towers. What belongs to the
portico on the ground floor belongs to the towers on

the upper floor — a Baroque ambiguity unexpected in the sedate classicism so far described.

In the interior the same emergence of Baroque conceptions within a dominant classicism can be observed. The nave for instance has — as was projected already in the pre-Fire design — saucer-domes and the fragmentary vaults for the apexes of the windows reach as penetrations towards the domes forming three-dimensional arches. Even more complex is the solution of the central space. Again on the pattern of what Wren had already considered in 1665-1666 and also in the warrant design the domed space has the width of nave and aisles put together. This generous widening at the crossing (Pl. 29) is the most remarkable effect of St. Paul's, an effect, to say it once again, derived from the so-called Octagon at Ely Cathedral. The dome is carred on eight arches, four large ones in the principal directions, and four smaller ones in the diagonals, which are ingeniously, if a little artificially, made to appear as large as the others. The diagonals thus consist of large niches on the lower floor with semispherical or aspidal vaults into which the aisles are conducted — and big broken segmental pediments over, and then, on the upper floor, balconies, or rather theatre boxes with segmental heads forming part of the apparent semi-circles to carry the dome. The dome rests on a drum and consists of three shells. The outer shell which so magnificently dominates the skyline of London is of timber, the inner shell is of stone, semicircular and open at the apex. Through it one looks into a semi-darkness where the only structurally essential middle shell disappears. This is of brick and conical in shape. It carries the splendidly Baroque stone lantern.

In the exterior of St. Paul's, just as in the City churches, Wren did not seek to achieve unity of style. There exists a contrast between the repose of the dome and the Baroque vivacity of the west towers, the one derived from Bramante (via Serlio), the other from Borromini's S. Agnese. Wren must have argued in his mind that the dome was to be the crowning achievement of the skyline of London, whereas the west towers would either be seen from a distance and then in conjunction with the many other church steeples in the neighborhood or from nearby, in which case the dome would not compete with them. So again uniformity is replaced by variety.

St. Paul's is not a building to evoke passionate reactions. It is the representation of an age which deprecated « enthusiasm » in the sense in which that term was then used by English churchmen. The interior indeed might have struck even them as a little chilly, if it had not been for the superb furnishings, woodwork, stone carving, and metalwork done with an artistry not inferior to any of the seventeenth century anywhere in Europe. The great iron worker was Jean Tijou whose most brilliant achievement are the ornamental gates in the gardens at Hampton Court (Pl. 35, 55), the great wood carver was Grinling Gibbons (Pl. 34), among the mason carvers the best were Jonathan Maine and Edward Pearce, the latter a sculptor of great skill in his own right, as is witnessed by his bust of Wren at the Ashmolean Museum in Oxford (Pl. 3). Wren here does not appear as in his late official painful portraits as the Surveyor General, but as the young, penetrating scientist, lively, intelligent and not without sensuality.

St. Paul's was begun in 1675. In 1677 the chancel and crossing were twenty-four feet up, and the transepts begun. So the idea of the semicircular porticoes of the transepts was early added to the warrant design. In the late eighties the nave and the west front (Pl. 30) were built, in fact, everything except the dome and the west towers (Pl. 31). For these the designs then contemplated were completely different from those executed. The projected dome (Pl. 32) was inspired by Michelangelo's at St. Peter's, the west towers by Bramante's Tempietto. In 1697 the choir was consecrated, but even in 1703 the final decision had not been taken on dome and west towers. They were finally built between 1705 and 1708. In 1711 the cathedral was declared complete.

Wren was seventy-nine years old then. It is a rare if not a unique case that one man should have designed a cathedral on this scale and have seen it achieved within his lifetime. That should give St. Paul's a unity over other cathedrals, but, as we have seen, Wren's own aesthetic theories were such that he changed as much in the course of the work and as drastically as later architects might have changed elsewhere. During the second half of the building operations Wren's relation to the supervising commission was not entirely happy. In 1697 a decision was taken to hold back half his salary until completion so as to speed up work. It was paid out only in 1711. One argument with the commission was because of their wish to see the cathedral finished on top by a balustrade. Wren evidently found this silly and wrote pointedly: « Ladies think nothing well without an edging. » But he does not seem to have minded much in the end — a sign of his wisdom, and indeed the balustrade does no damage to the design.

In 1714 the dynasty changed in England. George I represented a party hostile to the favorites of Queen Anne, and so in 1718 Wren was dismissed. He retired to a house he had bought himself by the river Thames at Hampton Court and wrote, with wisdom again, and with admirable resignation: « As I am dismissed, having worn out (by God's mercy) a long life in the Royal service, and having made some Figure in the World, I hope it will be allowed me to Die in peace. » He died in 1723.

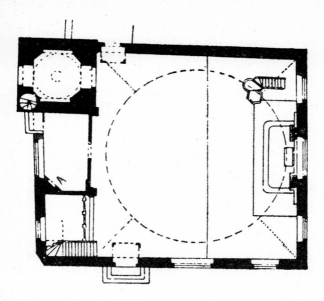

g) St. Mary Abchurch (being restored).

St. Paul's thus accompanied him through the major part of his life. On the City churches the bulk was done by the later eighties. After that there only followed some of the so far unexecuted spires (Pl. 12, 21), and they are as Baroque and fanciful as the west towers of St. Paul's. Most of what occupied Wren's time from the early eighties onwards was secular work. The client was as a rule the Court, although he also designed for his university friends, and occasionally for others, for instance the Middle Temple.

Among early secular work there was the former

Custom House built in 1668-1671, a simple design with giant pilasters and pediment on the Dutch pattern introduced into England by Hugh May at about the time when Wren began to take an interest in architecture. One year later, in 1669, when he became Surveyor General, he worked on a scheme for Whitehall Palace, following those proposed by John Webb, who was, as has been mentioned before, another older and more experienced architect. Nothing of this was executed. In the same year he designed a chapel with flanking ranges for Emmanuel College at Cambridge. The chapel front is decidedly more Baroque than that of Pembroke Chapel, and the lower flanking ranges have separate hipped roofs — resulting in a skyline broken as they liked them in France.

But much more important than this is another Cambridge job, the library for Trinity College (Pl. 40, 41). This was begun in 1676. Wren, fascinated just at that time by domed structures, first suggested a circular building, as he also suggested one in 1678 for a projected Mausoleum for Charles I, and somewhat later for a baptistery or chapter house west of St. Paul's Cathedral. This incidentally was part of a plan to surround St. Paul's by monumental ranges of buildings with colonnaded ground floors and giant pilasters above — on the pattern of the earliest of the squares of London, that designed by Inigo Jones at Covent Garden in the 1630s. Wren's design is strange in a very Wrenian way. Although it is symmetrical, it is not oval or rectangular or of any such simple type of shape. Instead of that the colonnaded ranges start with a semicircle then form a corner and run to the east tapering outward. They project behind the transepts forming another corner, and then again taper outward. The execution of the scheme would have combined formality with a picturesque variety of vistas as the shape of the cathedral brought it closer or less close to the colonnaded ranges. The scheme is undated but cannot be older than the eighties.

The circular plan for Trinity Library was not accepted, but when James Gibbs fifty years later built the famous Radcliffe Camera as part of the university library of Oxford he reverted to this type and developed it to far greater monumentality. Wren's Trinity Library is oblong, with one front closing an earlier courtyard at the far end of Trinity College, with the other facing the river Cam. That side is extremely severe, three giant doorways with Tuscan columns and no pediments, a tier of small windows between them and an upper tier of very large arched windows below a balustrade. The courtyard façade is more complex. Here the two stories have superimposed orders of attached columns, Tuscan and Ionic, and the openings are large and arched throughout. The general character has a calm and a nobility which had not yet been accessible to Wren when he designed the Sheldonian Theatre at Oxford thirteen years before. In fact the lower arches at the Trinity Library are a sham, like those referred to in the crossing at St. Paul's. Wren wanted the library room inside to gain the maximum of wall space and so illuminated the room from above. The upper windows, seen from inside, thus start much higher than one would assume from the exterior, and the actual area of the cubicles with desks and shelves against the walls and at right angles to them lie behind the entablature of the lower order and the sill-zone of the upper — a characteristically Baroque, contradictory interlocking of stories, noticed by Wren at Paris for instance in the Palais Mazarin. The balustrade as a crowning motif instead of a visible roof was to Wren a necessity for a monumental building. In the first of the four Tracts he wrote on architecture (and which were never published) he said: « No roof can have dignity enough to appear behind a cornice, but the circular. In private buildings it is excusable. »

But Wren designed few private buildings, though many have been attributed to him. Those that can be attributed to him with the greatest probability are extremely simple, of brick, with stone quoins, with plain windows and as a rule a pediment — the style in fact of May and which, as has already been said, was brought to England from Holland and later developed by many architects, masons and bricklayers, before and contemporary with Wren. A good example of this style is Morden College, at Blackheath, London (Pl. 42), an almshouse built in 1695 for a member of the commission responsible for the major work at the neighboring Greenwich Hospital, which began in 1698. Greenwich Hospital was for old or invalided sailors. A corresponding institution for soldiers had been established twelve years earlier at Chelsea in London, on the pattern of Louis XIV's recent Hôtel des Invalides.

Chelsea Hospital (Pl. 43-46) was built quickly and without changes in the execution. It is, like Wren's domestic buildings, of brick, as befitted a job which, though paid for by royal money, was for the housing of a humble population. The plan consists of long ranges along three sides of a courtyard open to the river Thames and some outbuildings. In the central range are the chapel on one side, the dining hall on the other of a circular entrance hall with a pretty lantern turret. The arrangement became accepted by Oxford Colleges a little later. It is also to be found on a more monumental scale in the south range of Tessin's Royal Palace at Stockholm begun in 1697. To the south and north the entrance hall has severe giant porticoes of four Tuscan columns. On the south side, along the sides of hall and chapel run low wooden colonnades with widely spaced coupled columns. The way they jut against the giant

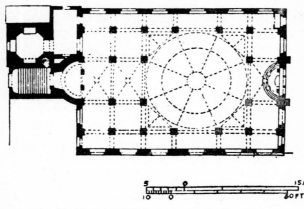

h) *St. Stephen Walbrook (restored after 1945)*.

portico is oddly careless. Such inelegancies occur every now and then in Wren's work. In their centers the side wings have porticoes of giant Doric pilasters, and these carry a pediment, broken and jutting back in the middle of the base — a Baroque motif, derived from Imperial Rome by way of France (Châtelet Chantilly, Mansart's Louvre designs). It stands at the beginning of a development of Wren's secular style towards more Baroque grandeur and drama.

The designs for a palace for Charles II at Winchester (Pl. 47), also with a deep *cour d'honneur,* and also with a few oddly Baroque motifs with giant orders, date from 1683. The palace was built rapidly but remained incompleted after Charles II died. It all but perished in a fire in the late nineteenth century. It was of brick too. Charles II died in 1685. His successor James II had only three years on the throne. He tried to reintroduce Catholicism and was expelled by the so-called Unbloody Revolution in 1688. His successor was William III or William of Orange, married to Mary, James II's daughter. Wren served them all, even James II for whom he designed a Council Chamber, a suite for the Queen and a Catholic chapel, all in Whitehall Palace. The main space of the chapel was an elongated octagon with three cross arms, a theme Wren had developed in the City churches too. But his greatest royal opportunities came with the accession of William and Mary. By then his former competitors had died, Webb in 1674, May in 1684, Pratt (who had retired long before) in 1685. Meanwhile, however, Wren had taken in as his chief assistant a young man, Nicholas Hawksmoor, who turned out to be immensely valuable as an amanuensis and in the end proved to be a great architect in his own right. How far the development of the late Wren style towards the cyclopic and Baroque was due to Hawksmoor, and how far it was the changing mood of Wren's own old age will probably never be fully clear. The problem is complicated by the emergence of yet another great architect about 1700, Sir John Vanbrugh. He was an amateur, like Wren, but of a very different character. He also was helped in his designs by Hawksmoor and became Comptroller of the Works under Wren, the Surveyor General, in 1702. Hawksmoor entered Wren's house and office much earlier, when he was only about eighteen years old, that is, ca. 1679. He became supervisor for Chelsea and Winchester, worked on the drawings for St. Paul's, and was made Clerk of the Works at Kensington Palace and Greenwich when work for William III started.

The date for the beginning at Kensington (Pl. 56, 61) is 1689; at Greenwich (Pl. 57-60), 1698. Work also started at Hampton Court (Pl. 48-55) in 1689. William III was asthmatic and did not wish to live at Whitehall or indeed in the smoke of London. So he wanted to make Hampton Court, a large rambling brick palace of the early sixteenth century, his principal seat, and Nottingham House at Kensington, a private house, then outside London, his suburban London seat.

Wren's original plans for Hampton Court were in competition with Versailles. He proposed to pull down the Tudor palace completely except for Henry VIII's Great Hall, and build an extensive *cour d'honneur* to the north with long side ranges for offices etc., and leading up at its far end to the old Hall. From here to the east a square block of four ranges around an inner courtyard was projected (like the Louvre) and west of this and the Hall another two ranges of outbuildings forming a record *cour d'honneur*. The center of the grand front was to have giant columns, a big attic and a dome. The scheme has been called French or Italian, but it is very English and Wrenish in that the Gothic hall of Henry VIII was going to be preserved, thus breaking the unity of style, and in that the groups of ranges were not to be developed along one main axis.

But William and Mary did not want anything so spectacular. So in the end a good deal of the Tudor work was allowed to remain and Wren only built the one large square courtyard, Fountain Court (Pl. 53), with its ranges of building around. The new work is of brick, as the Tudor palace had been, but with ample stone dressings. It is a homelike rather than a monumental effect, and that must have suited William and Mary well. Moreover, the main façades (Pl. 51, 52) are deprived of much of the monumentality which their size might have endowed them with by the odd arrangement of two attic stories above the piano nobile, one with circular, the other with square windows. This upper attic even kept the main pediment towards the formal, Versaillesque garden underneath. The whole of that center is somewhat cramped and uncomfortable. Sir Roger North, another amateur architect of the Wren circle — he designed the Middle Temple Gateway in the Dutch style — criticized it severely because « there is nothing rising at the angles, nor no large rising frontoon (i.e. pediment). » Wren was happier in the inner courtyard. Here all is more domestic, and the close placing of motifs helps to establish some intimacy in spite of the palatial scale. The ground floor arcades, incidentally, are another case of pretending to a different upper floor level than really exists.

Kensington Palace (Pl. 56) is even more frankly domestic. It is entirely of brick. Its general shape is irregular, its only slightly more formal façade has no more in the way of a principal accent than four giant pilasters and an attic with four vases standing above them.

The only time that Wren could really indulge in a monumentality that clearly haunted him was at Greenwich, and there — characteristically enough — not for a palace but for the naval hospital. Charles II had intended to build himself a truly royal palace here. As has been mentioned before, John Webb had been commissioned. His King Charles Block was begun in 1663. With its giant columns and pilasters it was the most Baroque and the most competently Baroque building of its date in England. It was meant to be one range of a composition with an identical range opposite and a main range at the far end across so that the whole would be open to the Thames. In 1692 William and Mary gave the site for the erection of a naval hospital to be as superior to Chelsea as the English navy was to the army. Wren began to make plans in 1694. After various suggestions for plan and elevation had been considered, construction began in 1698. The plan finally adopted is curious in its combination of monumentality with an avoidance of the obvious way in which monumentality would have been achieved in other countries. Wren kept King Charles Block and added an identical block opposite, just as Webb had intended, and again on the pattern of Webb, first intended to close his courtyard with a big range across. This was to have a dome and portico of giant angle pillars and columns *in antis* with low arcades jutting at it, similar to Chelsea though not so inorganically detailed. Then, however, it was decided that the Queen's Villa, lying a good deal further back from the river and built by Inigo Jones some eighty years before, should be made the central focal point of the composition. It was a strange decision, for Inigo Jones' masterpiece is extremely restrained, has hardly any relief, no giant motif, no dominating vertical accent and only a height of two stories. So Wren provided his own climax, and this is — again oddly unmonumental — two equal domed erections, as Baroque in the columns that surround the parts below the dome as are the late Wren church steeples. These two erections crown the entrances to the two main rooms, the hall and the chapel. The Chapel was internally remodeled in the late eighteenth century, the hall however remains, in the shape and with the decoration it was given between about 1705 and 1720. These two principal accents are visually connected by colonnades of coupled columns to King Charles Block and its opposite and identical but much longer colonnades run towards the Queen's Villa. They hide the utilitarian *raison d'être* of the whole composition, the dormitories of the pensioners. The whole is a spectacular procession of building, one of the grandest in England. The cool evenness of the colonnades remains in contrast to the crowding of columns in the towers — a contrast similar to that between dome and the west towers at St. Paul's. Wren did not see more completed at Greenwich than one of the two principal blocks with its dome and the colonnade of the other. In 1702 a new board of directors had been appointed to supervise the building work. Vanbrugh was a member, Hawksmoor, (from 1705) Deputy Surveyor. So some of the later work may be due to them. To Greenwich also belonged a garden going up the hill and laid out as early as 1664 in the Versailles manner, apperently by Le Nôtre himself.

In 1698, the year in which work started at Greenwich, a fire destroyed much of Whitehall Palace, including Wren's own work. Wren took the greatest trouble to save Inigo Jones' Banqueting House and was successful. After the fire he hoped for another opportunity to build a grand palace. The designs are in the style of Greenwich with heavy and steeply proportioned central four-column porticoes. One at least, the largest, which with a number of other drawings, only became known in 1951, is certainly not by Wren himself but by members of his staff. It has a long colonnade connecting it with a new House of Lords.

The contrast between the grandiose rhetoric of the designs for Whitehall and Greenwich and the simplicity of Kensington Palace or of Marlborough House built in 1708-1711 for the Duchess of Marlborough and the new chapter house for St. Paul's built in 1715 remains intriguing. The explanation is not that Wren himself was no longer responsible for the major jobs and left them to Hawksmoor and Vanbrugh, but that right through his life he had believed in different styles for different purposes. The Duchess of Marlborough hated the grandeur and cyclopic monumentality of Blenheim, the palace given by the nation to her celebrated husband and designed by Vanbrugh, and wanted a plain house to live in. The Chapter house of St. Paul's lies in the shadow of the cathedral and must not compete with it.

It was always the rationalism, the scepticism of Wren,

the scientist, which determined his decisions on style, his sense of what is proper for one job but not for another, his delight in experiment, or his latitudinarianism, to use a theological term. His never published four tracts on architectural theory have once before been quoted. Material for a fifth exists in a handwritten copy. Here he makes his views amply clear. They could not be more different from what, for instance, Bernini's or Mansart's must have been. Wren writes this: « Beauty, Firmness and Convenience are the Principles; the two first depend upon geometrical Reason of Opticks and Staticks; the third only makes the Variety... There are two Causes of Beauty — natural and customary. Natural is from Geometry, consisting of Uniformity (that is Equality) and Proportion. Customary Beauty is begotten by the Use of our Senses to those Objects which are usually pleasing to us for other Causes, a Familiarity or particular Inclination breeds a Love to Things not in themselves lovely. Here lies the great Occasion of Errors, here is tried the Architect's Judgement, but always the true test is Natural or Geometrical Beauty. Geometrical Figures are naturally more beautiful than the Irregular; in this all consent to a Law of Nature. Of geometrical Figures, the Square and the Circle are the most beautiful, next the Parallelogram and the Oval. Whatever a man's sentiments are upon mature consideration, it will be still necessary for him in a conspicuous work to accommodate his Design to the Gust of the Age he lives in, tho' it appear to him less rational. »

Here is uniformity and variety, Wren's faith in mathematics and his readiness to accommodate himself to customs and other people's tastes.

Nowhere does this attitude of Wren's appear more interestingly than in his reactions to the Gothic past of England. It has already been said that several of his church spires for the City of London are Gothic. There is even a completely Gothic interior, that of St. Mary Aldermary (Pl. 62), said to be a copy of the building which was burned, but evidently no more than a paraphrase. In addition the various Gothic features at St. Paul's have been emphasized, especially the flying buttresses. Church towers, with spires, are, moreover, a medieval motif altogether, unusual in Baroque Italy and France. What made Wren do these things? Was he unaware of the traditions he followed? No one should expect that from so alert and exeeedingly clear a mind. At the beginning of his career there was indeed not yet any ambiguity. In his memorandum of 1666 on the restoration of St. Paul's he suggested the modification to the old building to be « after the good Roman manner » rather than following « the Gothick Rudeness of the old Design. » But then, as he matured, his views changed, just as they had changed from the uniformity of the plan for London of 1666 to the variety of the City steeples. The most mature statement of his attitude toward the Gothic style is in letters of 1681 to Bishop Fell of Oxford, letters dealing with the completion of Tom Tower (Pl. 64), the gate tower of Christ Church, the most famous college of Oxford. This had been built at the same time as the Tudor parts of Hampton Court, and the gatehouse of typical Tudor style left incomplete. Wren completed it, with one broad domed tower in Gothic forms instead of the two flanking turrets intended. He writes first: « I resolved it ought to be Gothick to agree with the founder's work, but I have not continued so busy as he began... » Then however he deals with modifications which appeared necessary because an observatory was supposed to be built on the top of the tower. This, Wren says, would require a flat top and large straight-headed windows, and « such proportions as will not be reconcilable to the Gothick manner which spires up-

ward, and the pyramidal forms are essential to it...
This proposition had been much better effected had
not the parts formerly built diverted us from beginning
after the better Forms of Architecture, and I fear we
shall make an unhandsome medley this way. »

The same attitude Wren took much later, in 1713, when
he wrote a memorandum to the Dean of Westminster
Abbey on how the abbey of the thirteenth and fourteenth centuries ought to be completed which had (like
Wren's St. Paul's) at the beginning of the eighteenth
century still neither its west towers nor its intended
crossing tower. The former were in the end built by
Hawksmoor, the latter was never built. Wren's words
are: « I have made a Design... in the Gothick Form,
and of a Style with the Rest of the Structure: to
deviate from the old Form, would be to run into a
disagreeable Mixture, which no Person of good Taste
could relish... In like manner... I have among the Pa-
rochial Churches of London given some few Examples
(where I was obliged to deviate from a better style)
which appear not ungraceful, but ornamental. »

The most important passage in this is the last. So
Wren decided here and there in favor of Gothic by
taking in a very English way, « each case on its own
merit. » The decision might be taken in some cases in
order to conform with previous work, but in others it
must have been taken for the fun of it, that is, because
Wren enjoyed occasional excursions into strange styles.
The interior of St. Mary Aldemary (Pl. 62, 63) certainly must have given him pleasure.

This relativism may seem regrettable to many. For
it foreshadows clearly not only the philosophical scepticism of Hume and the aesthetic scepticism of Alison, but
also the attitude toward the choice of styles in the
Victorian Age. But it is not for the historian to regret.
For him what matters and what adds considerably to

Wren's historical significance is that Wren established an attitude which was to grow in the eighteenth century in England, to influence all other countries, and assume command internationally in the nineteenth — an attitude moreover which, in its tolerance and reasonableness, its abhorrence of the impossible, of absolutism, of « enthusiasm, » is eminently and eternally English.

AUTHOR'S NOTE

The preceding pages have little claim to originality. Most of what is found is based on the three best books in existence on the subject: Dr. Sekler's, Professor Webb's and Mr. Summerson's. What is the result of my own interpretation is the morphology of the city churches and the interpretation of Wren's attitude to the choice of styles.

The systematic description of the plans and the steeples of the city churches is taken from the introduction to my volume on the *Cities of London and Westminster* in *The Buildings of England*, Penguin Books, 1956. The drawings of the steeples are reproduced by permission of Mr. Gerald Cobb from his excellent little book, *London City Churches*, 1951, printed by the Corporation of London. The plans of city churches are from Dr. Sekler's book and reproduced by the kindness of Messrs. Faber & Faber. Nearly all the photographs were taken especially for the book by Mr. Roger Mayne; photographs numbered 40 and 41 are by A. F. Kersting and number 25 by W. G. Davis.

BIOGRAPHY

1632 - *Birth of Christopher Wren in the village of Knoyle (Wiltshire).*

1651 - *Received a Master of Arts from Oxford.*

1657 - *Named Professor of Astronomy at Gresham College, London.*

1661 - *Named Professor of Astronomy at Oxford.*

1663 - *Presented the project for the Sheldonian Theatre, his first architectural work, to the Royal Society.*

1664-1665 - *Commissioned by King Charles II to report on the condition of St. Paul's Cathedral, London.*

1665 - *Left for Paris.*

1666 - *In September a fire destroyed three quarters of London.*
A few days after the fire Wren presented a project for the reconstruction of London based on the principle of the rond-point with radiating streets. This revolutionary plan was never accepted.

1672-1686 - *Of the eighty-seven churches destroyed by the fire Wren rebuilt fifty.*

1675 - *Approval of the final plans for the complete reconstruction of St. Paul's, which was badly damaged by the fire.*
He is knighted and takes the title of Sir.

1676 - *Beginning of Trinity College Library at Oxford.*

1683 - *Project for the palace at Winchester.*

1686 - *Beginning of Chelsea Hospital.*

1689 - *Beginning of work at Kensington and at Hampton Court.*

1694 - *Preparations for Greenwich Hospital.*

1698 - *Beginning of work on Greenwich Hospital.*

1718 - *With the change in dynasty Wren is dismissed.*

1723 - *Death of Wren.*

BIBLIOGRAPHY

S. WREN, *Parentalia*, London, 1750.

Wren's Society (edited by A.T. Bolton and H.D. Hendry), 20 vols., London, 1924-1943.

G. WEBB, *Sir Christopher Wren*, London, 1937.

J. SUMMERSON, *Sir Christopher Wren*, London, 1951.

E. SEKLER, *Wren and his Place in European Architecture*, London, 1956.

To the above must be added the following works on Wren's drawings:

J. SUMMERSON, *Preliminary publication and interpretation of drawings found in 1951*, « The Times, » Oct. 11, 1951 and « Journal of the Royal Institute of British Architects, » Feb. 1952.

V. FÜRST's, *The Architecture of Sir Christopher Wren*, London, 1956, can be recommended only with reservation. Its principal merit is the discussion of Wren's drawings. It also contains a list of most of the books which Wren possessed and a work catalog. In addition Mr. Fürst as well as Dr. Sekler give long bibliographies.

ILLUSTRATIONS

2

Oxford - Sheldonian Theatre (1663-1669).

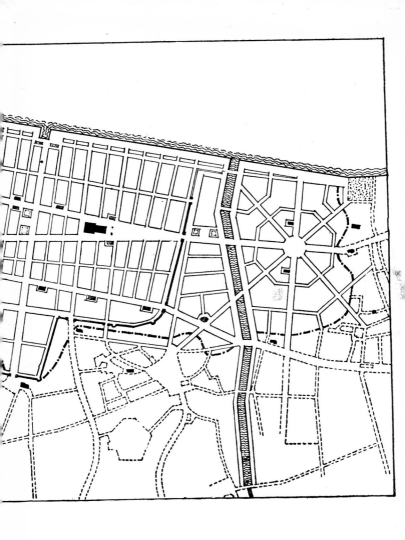

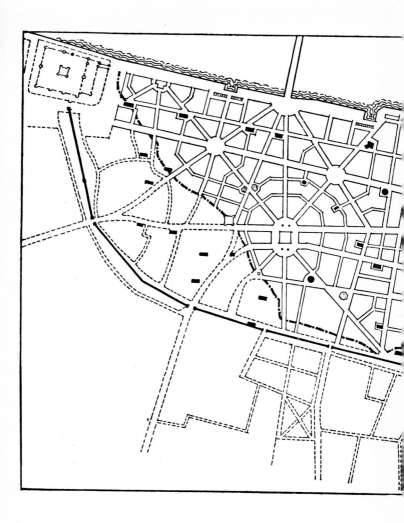

1 - Wren's plan for the reconstruction of London (1666).

3

Oxford, Ashmolean Museum - Bust of Wren by Edward Pearce.

4

St. James Garlickhithe - The tower.

5

St. James, Piccadilly - Interior.

6

St. Magnus - Interior.

7

St. Mary Abchurch - Interior.

8

St. Martin Ludgate - Interior.

9
St. Stephen Walbrook - Interior.

10

St. Peter Cornhill - East façade.

11

St. Mary Aldermanbury - East façade.

12

St. Bride - Bell tower.

13

St. Mary-le-Bow - Bell tower (Cheapside).

14

Christ Church, Newgate Street - Bell tower.

15
St. Magnus - Bell tower.

16

St. Martin Ludgate - Bell tower.

17

St. Stephen Walbrook - Bell tower.

18

St. Michael Paternoster Royal - Bell tower.

19

St. Vedast - Bell tower.

20

St. Margaret Pattens - Bell tower.

21

St. Dunstan-in-the-East - Bell tower.

22

St. Paul's Cathedral - Plan before the fire (ca. 1666).

23

St. Paul's Cathedral - Plan with Greek cross (ca. 1673).

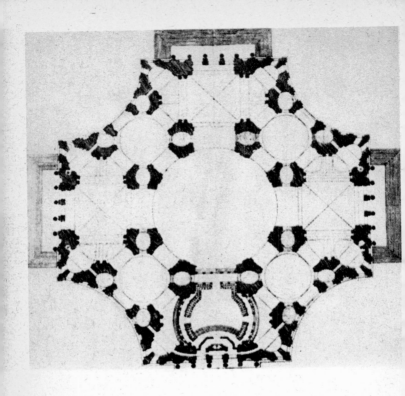

24

St. Paul's Cathedral - Plan with Greek cross.

25

St. Paul's Cathedral - The great model (1673).

26

St. Paul's Cathedral - Final plan (1675).

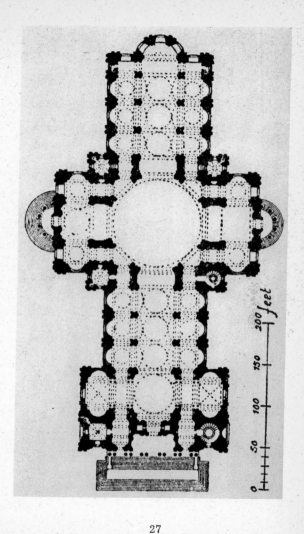

27

St. Paul's Cathedral - Drawing (1675-1711).

28
St. Paul's Cathedral - Interior.

29
St. Paul's Cathedral - Detail of the arches of the crossing.

30

St. Paul's Cathedral - West façade.

31

St. Paul's Cathedral - West towers (1705-1708).

32
St. Paul's Cathedral - Dome (1705-1708).

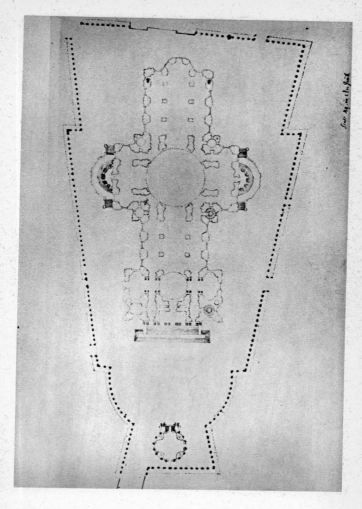

33

St. Paul's Cathedral - Plan with colonnades and five-story houses.

34

St. Paul's Cathedral - Interior decoration. Choir stalls by Grinling
Gibbons.

35

St. Paul's Cathedral - Interior decoration. Doors to the choir by
Jean Tijou.

36

Decorations for churches - Retable of St. Magnus.

37

Decorations for churches - Pulpit and plaster ornaments
at St. Stephen Walbrook.

38

Decorations for churches - Pulpit at St. Stephen Walbrook.

Decorations for churches - Pulpit at St. Mary Aldermary.

40

Cambridge, Trinity College - The library seen from the river (started in 1676).

41

Cambridge, Trinity College - The library seen from Neville's Court.

42

London, Blackheath - Morden College (1695).

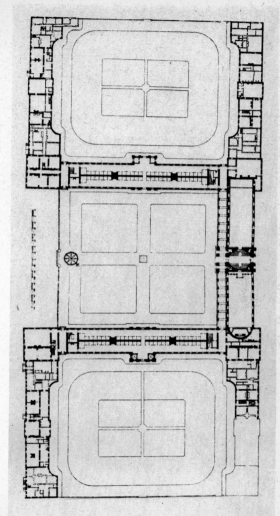

43

Chelsea Hospital
n (started in 1682).

44

Chelsea Hospital, seen from the road.

45

Chelsea Hospital, seen from the river.

46

Chelsea Hospital - The great hall seen from the entrance.

47

Winchester Palace (started in 1683).

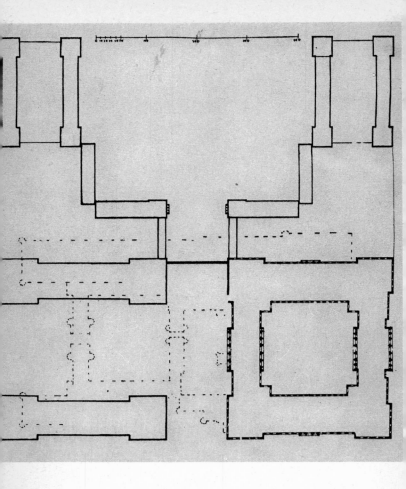

48

Hampton Court (started in 1689) - First plan.

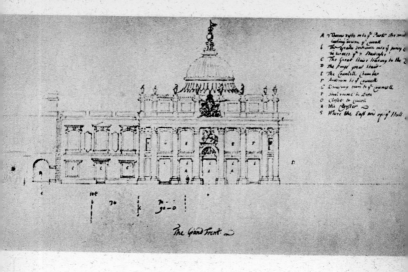

Hampton Court (started in 1689) - Side view, first plan.

50

Hampton Court - **Exterior.**

51

Hampton Court - Center of the south façade.

Hampton Court - Center of the east façade.

53

Hampton Court - Court of the fountain.

54

Hampton Court - Door.

55

Hampton Court - Detail of wrought iron doors by Jean Tijou.

56

Kensington Palace (started in 1689).

57
Greenwich Hospital - View from the park.

58
Greenwich Hospital - Charles I wing by John Webb (started in 1663).

59

Greenwich Hospital - Colonnade and dome of the chapel (started in 1698).

60

Greenwich Hospital - Colonnade.

61

Kensington Palace - The orangery (started in 1704) according to the plans of Wren or Sir John Vanbrugh.

62

St. Mary Aldermary - Interior.

63
St. Mary Aldermary - The vault.

64

Oxford - Tom Tower (started in 1681).

INDEX OF ILLUSTRATIONS